Writing for Business Results

Writing for Business Results

PATRICIA E. SERAYDARIAN

The Business Skills Express Series

BUSINESS ONE IRWIN/MIRROR PRESS
Burr Ridge, Illinois

© RICHARD D. IRWIN, INC., 1994

This publication is designed to provide accurate and authoritative information in regard to the subject matter covered. It is sold with the understanding that neither the author nor the publisher is engaged in rendering legal, accounting, or other professional service. If legal advice or other expert assistance is required, the services of a competent professional person should be sought.

From a Declaration of Principles jointly adopted by a Committee of the American Bar Association and a Committee of Publishers.

Mirror Press:	David R. Helmstadter
	Carla F. Tishler
Editor-in-Chief:	Jeffrey A. Krames
Project editor:	Stephanie M. Britt
Production manager:	Diane Palmer
Designer:	Jeanne M. Rivera
Art coordinator:	Heather Burbridge
Illustrator:	Boston Graphics, Inc.
Compositor:	Alexander Graphics
Typeface:	12/14 Criterion
Printer:	Malloy Lithographing, Inc.

Library of Congress Cataloging-in-Publication Data

Seraydarian, Patricia E., 1934-
    Writing for business results / Patricia E. Seraydarian.
        p.   cm.—(Business skills express)
    ISBN 1-55623-854-1
    1. Business writing.   2. English language—Business English.
    I. Title.   II. Series.
    HF5718.3.S44   1994
    808'.06665—dc20   92–41874
                                                                              Rev.

Printed in the United States of America
    2 3 4 5 6 7 8 9 0 ML 0 9 8 7 6 5 4 3

PREFACE

Have you ever thought, "I wish I were a better writer"? Or perhaps, "I wish I felt more confident that my writing is effective." Wherever you fall on the scale of writing skills, this book is designed for you.

If you are just beginning your career and need basic help with your business writing, you will find the principles of good business writing in succinct, clear language. If you are an experienced writer who needs a refresher, you will find your skills reinforced and enhanced with this presentation.

How can you get the most out of this book? Begin by completing the Self-Assessment. This will help you establish your present position. Then work through each of the five chapters. While the entire book can be completed in one to two hours, I recommend that you do one chapter at each sitting. This will help you focus on a single topic. When you have been through the chapters, take the Post-Test. You will be surprised at how much you have learned.

You will be so pleased with your results that you will want to measure your progress over a period of time. Completing the Skill Maintenance checklist will do that for you. When you finish Chapter 5, be sure to enter the date on the checklist. Then follow the instructions and measure your growth over a year.

Good luck. You have taken the first step to improved writing. Turn the page and continue the journey.

Patricia E. Seraydarian

ABOUT THE AUTHOR

Patricia E. Seraydarian is the president and principal trainer of C-TIP, Inc., in Las Vegas, Nevada. She has had extensive professional experience as a consultant and trainer in corporate, government, and academic settings. A member of many professional organizations, she is the author of more than a dozen books. Her clients include Michigan Consolidated Gas Company, Livonia Public Schools, and the Business Technology Center of Oakland Community College. Dr. Seraydarian received her Ph.D. from the University of Michigan.

ABOUT
BUSINESS ONE IRWIN

Business One Irwin is the nation's premier publisher of business books. As a Times Mirror company, we work closely with Times Mirror training organizations, including Zenger-Miller, Inc., Learning International, Inc., and Kaset International to serve the training needs of business and industry.

About the Business Skills Express Series

This expanding series of authoritative, concise, and fast-paced books delivers high quality training on key business topics at a remarkably affordable cost. The series will help managers, supervisors, and front line personnel in organizations of all sizes and types hone their business skills while enhancing job performance and career satisfaction.

Business Skills Express books are ideal for employee seminars, independent self-study, on-the-job training, and classroom-based instruction. Express books are also convenient-to-use references at work.

CONTENTS

Self-Assessment

How do you feel about your business writing ability? The simple self-assessment that follows may confirm your confidence or may suggest areas for improvement. In either case, it will provide a starting point for you as you begin *Writing for Business Results*.

	Almost Always	Sometimes	Almost Never
1. I feel very confident when writing letters and memos.	_____	_____	_____
2. Getting started when writing is easy for me.	_____	_____	_____
3. I feel very confident that the format of my letters conforms to standard practices.	_____	_____	_____
4. I always plan before writing.	_____	_____	_____
5. I feel sure my opening paragraphs capture the attention of my reader.	_____	_____	_____
6. I gather all my information and check any necessary details before writing.	_____	_____	_____
7. I am careful to state what I want the reader to do.	_____	_____	_____
8. My letters always close with a clincher.	_____	_____	_____
9. I limit my letters and memos to one page if possible.	_____	_____	_____
10. I limit my paragraphs to single ideas.	_____	_____	_____
11. My electronic messages always get results.	_____	_____	_____
12. The five C's of business writing (conciseness, completeness, courtesy, clarity, correctness) are always identifiable in my writing.	_____	_____	_____
13. I am confident the spelling and grammar in my documents are always correct.	_____	_____	_____
14. I consciously avoid redundant expressions, jargon, cliches, and sexism in my writing.	_____	_____	_____
15. I wish I could improve my business writing skills.	_____	_____	_____

1 Letters

This chapter will help you to:

- Understand why you write letters.
- Plan your writing for success.
- Write each part of the letter to achieve the desired result.
- Format correspondence to project a contemporary image.

Jose Carlos is a very careful writer. He puts considerable time and effort into the many letters he writes during a normal business day. However, he often feels frustrated because his readers either do not respond or they call for additional information. Sometimes he wonders why he works so hard at writing. He suspects that much of his correspondence is not even read.

If this sounds familiar, then Chapter 1 is written just for you. ■

UNDERSTANDING WHY YOU WRITE LETTERS

Have you ever asked yourself why you write letters? Perhaps you think that is a foolish question. The truth is, most of us write without ever asking this critical question. Perhaps we don't ask the question because the answer is obvious: We write to get results.

The next question is, how often do your letters bring the desired results? Almost always, usually, or less often than you wish? What are the secrets of successful business letters—letters that get results?

FOUR CRITICAL QUESTIONS

You can write letters that bring results if you answer four questions before you begin to write.

Why Am I Writing?

What is your reason for writing? The majority of business letters are written for one of the following purposes:

- To convey information.
- To invite or respond.
- To inquire or request.
- To express appreciation or regret.
- To remind.
- To move to action.

If you cannot identify a specific purpose for writing, perhaps you don't need to write a letter. A phone call or a visit might achieve your goals.

To Whom Am I Writing?

What do you know about your reader? When you know the personality of your reader, you have the advantage of tailoring your letter. When you don't know your reader, or when your reader is part of a generic group (i.e., clients or customers), you must write your letters to communicate a warm human element.

What Information or Message Must I Convey?

Have your facts in order before you begin to write. Eliminate unnecessary or nice-to-know information. Focus on the main message.

What Results Do I Want?

What do you want your reader to do? How do you want your reader to respond? If you don't know, your reader won't know either.

■ Review & Practice

Read the text of the letter on the next page. Answer each of the following questions.

Why was the letter written? Refer to the reasons for writing above. Which one applies to this letter?

_____

How well do you think the writer knows the reader?

Very well _____ Somewhat acquainted _____ Not personally
acquainted _____ Not at all _____

> Dear Ms. Portfena:
>
> The National Association of Women Entrepreneurs is holding its annual meeting January 15–18, 199–, in New Orleans. As one of the most successful entrepreneurs in the United States, we would like to invite you to be the keynote speaker at our closing banquet on January 18 at 6:30 P.M. in the Magnolia Ballroom of the Bayou Plaza Hotel.
>
> My assistant, Gladys Abdul, will call you next week to determine if this date is available and if you can accept the invitation.
>
> We need to complete our planning within the next 30 days. On behalf of the planning committee, I want to express the eagerness of each of us to have you participate in our meeting.
>
> Sincerely,

Does the letter convey a warm, human element?

Yes _____   No _____   Not certain _____

What information was necessary? List the facts needed by the reader.

_____   _____

_____   _____

What results does the writer want? List the results the writer is seeking.

_____   _____

_____   _____

The solution appears on page 87.

Hints

Prescription for Writer's Block

The cure for writer's block is to *begin writing*. Use your letter plan and write a first draft. If time permits, put it aside and revise it later. The most experienced writers will tell you they write, rewrite, and write again—before writing the final copy.

PLANNING THE LETTER

Every successful letter begins with a plan. The plan may be a formal outline or, more typically, an informal list of the contents.

Planning your letter involves three steps:

Begin writing here.

Step 3: Fill in the details.

Step 2: Arrange the points in appropriate sequence.

Begin planning here.
↓

Step 1: List the two or three major points to be covered.

1

■ R e v i e w & P r a c t i c e

Last Friday you completed a three-session training seminar entitled "Career Planning for the Year 2000" at your local community college. You need to write a letter verifying your attendance for your personnel file. Write your letter plan.

Step 1: List the major points to be covered. (Four lines are provided; you may have fewer or more points.)

_____

_____

_____

_____

Step 2: Number the items you listed above in the order in which they will appear in the letter by writing 1, 2, 3, or 4, in the space at the left of each line.

Step 3: Since this is only practice, you will skip Step 3—filling in the details—in this exercise. In actual practice, you will always complete this step before you begin to write.

A sample solution appears on page 87.

LETTER PARTS

Most letters contain either three or four parts, as appropriate:

- An opening or introduction.
- The main message.
- A statement of results desired.
- The closing.

The Opening

Four critical seconds—business correspondence specialists tell us that's how long you have to get the attention of your reader.

The opening must get the attention of the reader. It contains your topic sentence—your reason for writing. A dull opening suggests a dull letter—one that may not even be read, let alone generate a response.

Weak Openings	Improved Openings
We have received your letter of June 25, 199–, confirming your plans to speak to our group.	Thank you for confirming your plans to speak to our group.
Obvious fact. If you had not received a letter, would you be writing this letter?	Combines a warm thank-you with a brief statement of the purpose of the letter.
This letter is to inform you of the upcoming Executive Committee meeting.	The Executive Committee will meet on Thursday, July 27, at 2 P.M. in the Spring Mountain Room of the Southwest Hotel.
Don't talk about it—do it!	Gives the reader all the important facts in the first paragraph.
We have made attempts to collect the past due amount on your account.	We are frustrated! We have tried unsuccessfully to collect the $159.15 owed us on your account #7QR54.
A good beginning but leaves out the facts.	An unusual opening that is sure to catch the attention of the reader. Leaves no doubt in the reader's mind about the purpose of the letter.

The Main Message

The main message contains all the necessary information and details you need to convey. It can be taken directly from a carefully written letter plan.

Weak Main Messages	Improved Main Messages
Jane Doe was an honors student at Summerlin College during the late 1980s and early 1990s.	Jane Doe attended Summerlin College from September 1988 through June 1992. She graduated magna cum laude from the School of Education.
Verifies the fact that she was enrolled at the college but gives few additional—and needed—details.	Gives detailed information about Jane's college experience.
Leo Fritelli is a former employee of Magna Corporation. His work was always excellent.	Leo Fritelli was employed by Magna Corporation as a systems analyst from June 15, 1985, to September 30, 1989. Leo's individual work was always superior, and his teamwork was excellent. We were sorry to lose Leo, but we understood his reasons for seeking another position.

(continued)

1

(concluded)

Verifies his employment without giving any details. Would not be helpful to a potential employer.	Gives detailed information about Leo's employment. Adds a warm, personal note in the final sentence.

The Action or Results

When appropriate, state what information you are seeking or what results you desire. Be specific. Do not leave your reader wondering what it is you want.

Request for Action or Results	Improved Requests
Please confirm your appointment as soon as possible	Please confirm your appointment by calling my administrative assistant at Extension 2655 no later than Friday, July 15.
States request vaguely. Does not give the reader the information needed to comply with the request.	States the action desired in definite terms.
The preliminary audit report would be helpful at our meeting next week.	Plan to bring the preliminary audit report with you when we meet with the comptroller next week.
Suggests possible action rather than makes a firm request.	States specifically what is needed and when it is needed.

The Closing

The closing of your letter may take any of several forms, as determined by the nature of the letter. It may be a summary of the major ideas, a simple statement of good will, or a clincher to motivate the reader.

Weak Closings	Improved Closings
Thank you in advance	Thanks so much for your patience in this matter.
A presumptuous closing. Never assume the reader's action.	Combines an always appropriate thank-you with a specific comment.
You can order this special communications package by calling us today.	A phone call from you will enable you to enjoy the advantages of on-line communications immediately.

(continued)

(concluded)

| The reader knows the product is available. This closing does nothing to clinch the deal. | This closing has the reader in mind. It's to the reader's advantage to place an order— a good clincher. |

THE APPEARANCE OF YOUR LETTERS

Marissa Nenadvich is a skilled letter writer. She carefully plans each letter before she writes it. She always reads her letters to be certain she has included all pertinent information. She makes a concentrated effort to stress the reader's point of view and writes with warm tones. Yet, she often fails to get results, particularly when writing to persons she does not know.

She took several samples of her writing to a communications consultant, who promptly identified her problem—the appearance of her letters. She was puzzled because the format of her letters is consistent with the format of letters found in her predecessor's files. Marissa soon learned that her formatting skills were outdated. ■

Someone once said, "You never get a second chance to make a first impression." That statement is true of your letters.

Writing for results involves not only the contents of the letter but also the appearance of the letter. Some readers may make a decision on whether or not to read your letter and respond to it solely on how it looks. Whether you are the originator of the letter or the support staff person who keys and prints the document, you must be aware of how a letter should look if it is to bring results.

PROJECTING A CONTEMPORARY IMAGE

What is appropriate formatting for today's business letters? What recent style changes can you incorporate into your letters to enhance their overall appearance? How can you send a nonverbal message that says you understand that both appearance and content contribute to successful business writing? These suggestions will help you.

- Your letters should be consistent with one of the styles illustrated on pages 12 and 13.

- The date should appear in the following order: *January 1, 199–*. The military form *1 January 199–* is appropriate only for military or international correspondence.

- The salutations *Dear Sir* and *Gentlemen* are dated. *Dear Sirs* is never used. Use the addressee's name or title, for example, *Dear Mr. Thomas,* or *Dear Manager,* whenever possible. When writing to a group, *Ladies and Gentlemen* is the accepted salutation.

- Single-space the body of the letter; double-space between paragraphs. Indent text paragraphs only if you are observing the

1

modified block style. Listings and enumerated items may be indented one tab stop from the left margin.

- The name of the writer's company is not included in the closing lines since it appears in the letterhead.

- Less formal closings, such as *Sincerely* rather than *Respectfully*, are preferred.

- Only the typist's initials in lowercase are included in the reference notation, not the writer's. The notation should read *abc* not *JBK/abc*.

- Copy notations should reflect the use of photocopiers rather than carbon paper, reading *c, copy,* or *pc* rather than *cc*.

FORMAT STYLES

Letter formats should be consistent with one of the two styles shown on these pages. Most people are more familiar with the modified block style.

BLOCK STYLE LETTER

BAY VIEW CONSULTANTS
4750 Landsdowne Place - Suite 555
Annapolis, MD 21401

(410) 770-2010   FAX (410) 770-2015

May 25, 199—

The Norris Agency
3330 Riverside Drive
Baltimore, MD 21295

Ladies and Gentlemen

Thank you for your letter of May 23, 199—, confirming our appointment on June 2, 199—, in your offices. You will be pleased to learn that Shultua Liang, our executive vice president who has a strong interest in your agency, plans to join us.

We will prepare the following items for our meeting:

- Proposal for the new Norris advertising campaign.
- Preliminary artwork for the campaign.
- Detailed information on the timeliness for the campaign..

We think you will be very excited when you see this proposal. It is uniquely Norris and will enhance the positive image you already enjoy in the advertising world.

Sincerely

M. G. Ashton
Executive Director

lkj

- All lines begin at the left.
- The date begins approximately one inch below the letterhead—this position is adjusted for very short or very long letters.
- Open punctuation is used—no colon after the salutation and no comma after the closing.
- A listing begins at the left margin or is indented.

MODIFIED BLOCK LETTER

METROPLEX MEDICAL ASSOCIATES, P.C.
4500 Professional Plaza
Forth Worth, TX 76123

(817) 363-1950   FAX (817) 363-1951

May 25, 199–

Massena Pharmaceuticals
P.O. Box 224
Massena, NY 13662

Ladies and Gentlemen:

Thank you for the prompt shipment of our order No. 3625–P. However, in checking the contents of the order, we find the following discrepancies:

15 doz. Super-X gloves ordered	10 doz. received
10 doz. No. 15 bandages	15 doz. received

Invoice No. 45-PQ-3459, enclosed with the order, lists the items as we ordered them. Rather than adjust the shipment at this point, would you please adjust the invoice to reflect the shipment as received and send us a corrected copy.

Sincerely,

Rose Levine
Office Manager

ytt

- The date and closing lines begin at center.
- Standard punctuation is used—a colon after the salutation and a comma after the complimentary close.
- Paragraphs may be blocked or indented.

PUTTING IT ALL TOGETHER

Now that you have reviewed the basic principles of planning and writing business letters, it is time to put your new skill to work. Refer to the preceding pages as often as you need to. First prepare a letter plan for the situation described on page 14, and then compose the paragraphs of the letter.

Situation: Write a letter in response to a customer who requests information on the newest version of the software developed by your company. The new version will not be available until early next year and will include many enhancements suggested by current users. Pricing information is not available at this time.

Use the space below to prepare your letter plan.

_____

Did you remember to sequence the items?

You may wish to prepare a first draft on a separate sheet of paper. This page may be used for the final copy.

1

_____
_____
_____
_____
_____
_____
_____
_____
_____
_____
_____
_____
_____
_____
_____
_____
_____
_____
_____
_____
_____
_____
_____
_____
_____
_____
_____
_____
_____
_____
_____
_____

You will find a sample solution on page 88. This solution is only a suggested one. Look at the points the suggested letter makes. Compare them to those in your letter.

Chapter Checkpoints

Writing Checkpoints

✓ Did you begin with a writing plan?

✓ Did you limit each paragraph to one major idea?

✓ When possible, did you limit paragraphs to five or six lines each?

✓ Have you used listings for lengthy details rather than narratives?

✓ Did you remember that one-page letters are always preferable?

✓ Did you check all details before writing the final copy?

Formatting Checkpoints

✓ Scan the letter. Is it placed attractively on the page? Does it appear balanced with your letterhead? Clue: Use the center page feature of your software.

✓ Did you use the default margins of your software (usually one inch)?

✓ Is the format consistent with one of the two accepted styles—block or modified block?

✓ What is the readability quotient of your letter? Does it include:

Short paragraphs?

A single, clear typeface?

A ragged right margin?

Lots of white space?

2 | Interoffice Memos

This chapter will help you to:

- Develop your "memo image."
- Write memos with a purpose.
- Master the principles of successful memo writing.
- Transmit effective electronic messages.

Curtis Harrera, office manager of Superior Office Products, writes several memos every day. In fact, since his responsibilities are internal, he seldom writes a letter.

Recently he distributed a memo that contained some very important information. Later he overheard two of his employees talking: "Doesn't Curtis have anything else to do but write memos? They are always so long!" The second employee replied, "I've learned to glance at the subject line; if I think it's a 'must read,' I do. Otherwise, it goes in my 'do later' pile. Someone should just tell him that enough is enough!"

This scene is repeated in too many offices every day. Are your memos taken seriously? Chapter 2 will help you take a critical look at your memo-writing practices and provide you with guidelines to increase the acceptability factor of your memos. ■

MEMOS—WE GET MEMOS!

Do you find that you read and write more memos than letters? If so, you are typical of today's business writer.

Do you feel confident that you can write a memo that commands attention and gets results? Since memos represent internal communication, they tend to accumulate in other people's files, including those of your superiors. What is the memo image of your file?

Is your image fresh? Does a glance at your memos invite reading? Does the content of your memos convey conciseness, preciseness, inclusiveness, and warmth? Or are your memos dull? Are they wordy, indefinite, stilted, and even unnecessary?

FORMATTING THE MEMO

Your memo image begins with the appearance of the memo. Apply these checkpoints to the sample memo below.

- Is it one page in length?
- Are related items aligned?
- Are the paragraphs short?
- If you scan the memo, does it look readable—and thus invite reading?
- When appropriate, have you used a list format rather than a narrative?
- Does it contain as much white space as possible?

MEMORANDUM

TO: Yehuda Vitko
FROM: Gilbert Koslov
DATE: August 9, 199–
SUBJECT: RENO BPW MEETING

Thanks so much for agreeing to speak to the Reno BPW convention on October 15, 199–. The members of this group are true professionals, and you will find this opportunity a delightful challenge.

The details are:

Reno Business and Professional Women.

Admirals Hotel—Marina Room.

October 15, 199–.

12 noon closing luncheon.

20-minute presentation on a topic of your choice.

Your contact person, Joyce Chung, will call you within the next few days.

jjk

Did you notice that you can answer each of these checkpoints simply by scanning the memo, without having to read it? That's what image means— a first impression.

2

PLANNING THE MEMO

Interoffice memos may be printed on plan paper or printed forms. In either case, four items always appear. Printed forms may have additional fill-in lines.

- The name of the addressee(s).
- The name of the originator.
- The date the memo is written.
- The subject of the memo.

Checkpoints for Memo Details

- When a memo is being sent to several people, replace individual names with a *Distribution List.* List names of recipients below the last line of the message. (The memo on page 21 illustrates this feature.)
- Usually place the names in a distribution list in alphabetical order. You may place names in order of seniority or rank within the organization. Caution: A ranked list leaves open the possibility of misplacing a name.
- Do not use job titles in memos.
- Use a descriptive subject line.
- Replace the signature line by the handwritten initials of the originator at the top of the memo.

PREPARING TO WRITE THE MEMO

Effective writing always begins with planning. Planning begins when you answer one critical question:

What do I want the reader to know or do after reading this memo?

■ R e v i e w   &   P r a c t i c e

Read the following memo. Underline what the writer wants the reader to know. Place a check mark beside what the writer wants the reader to do after reading the memo.

2

ABC Interoffice MEMO

TO: Distribution List

FROM: Shirley Kyte

DATE: March 22, 199–

SUBJECT: IRS RULING—TRAVEL REIMBURSEMENT

On March 1, 199–, the IRS ruled (Opinion #345-QR) that all travel reimbursements must be included in the employee's tax forms as nontaxable compensation.

Please act immediately to add such reimbursements to the records of all employees to be included in the end-of-year reporting.

ert

Distribution:
A. Abrams
K. Chin
L. Jabbar
B. Kahookaulana

See the sample solution on page 88.

■ H i n t s ──────────────

Writing is easy . . . when you remember:

Determining your purpose for writing **precedes** preparing a writing plan, which **precedes** writing a first draft, which **precedes** writing a final copy.

Once you have determined what you want the reader to know or do, you are ready to plan the memo. Planning is a three-step process:

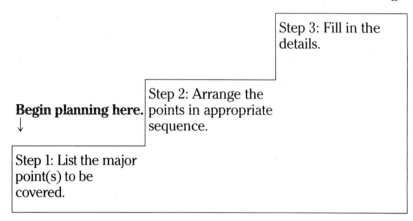

Begin writing here.

Step 3: Fill in the details.

Step 2: Arrange the points in appropriate sequence.

Begin planning here.
↓

Step 1: List the major point(s) to be covered.

▮ Review & Practice

Kaye Sanchez, mail supervisor for Southwest Products, must write a memo to initiate the following three changes in mailing procedures: Mail to be sent by a private carrier must be received by 3:30 P.M. Overnight mail must be received by 4:00 P.M. Mail must be received in the mail room by 4:30 P.M. to be mailed the same day. These changes are to take effect July 15.

Step 1: List the major points to be covered. (Four lines are provided; you may have fewer or more points.)

_____

_____

_____

_____

Step 2: Number the points you listed above in sequence by writing 1, 2, 3, or 4, in the space at the left of each line above.

Step 3: Since this is a practice exercise, you will skip Step 3—filling in the details—in this exercise. In actual practice, always complete this step before you begin to write.

A sample solution appears on page 88.

WRITING THE MEMO

Memo Secrets

Put the message up front.

The Opening

The most important information in your memo, including conclusions or recommendations, belongs in the first sentence or paragraph.

Writing in this way captures the attention of your reader immediately and makes your reason for writing clear. It sets the stage for action or decisions.

Read the following opening paragraph:

Sometimes big corporations are accused of being indifferent to human needs. I think that is why I was so pleased to learn of a recent series of events that involved a group of our employees in the Dayton plant.

What important information is conveyed in this paragraph? Does it really grab your interest? Or, do you respond in a "Ho hum, that's nice" manner? How would you respond to the paragraph below if you received this memo in the middle of a hectic day in which everything had gone wrong?

Verna White, a maintenance technician in our Dayton plant who found herself and her six children homeless just six months ago, is a proud new homeowner—thanks to the efforts of 23 of her co-workers.

Would you agree that this opening paragraph is more intriguing, leading you to continue reading? The main point is in the first paragraph.

Memo Secrets

Say only what is necessary.

2

The Main Message

The succeeding paragraphs of your memo briefly support the important information already conveyed in the first paragraph. Only pertinent information is included. Nice-to-know information does not have a place in memos.

Listings may be used very effectively with some types of information. Compare the following main message paragraphs of a memo.

You might wish to consider the following topics as you plan your presentation: Quality Circles, Management with Meaning, The Corporate Ladder Has a Missing Rung, You Ain't There Yet!, or High Tech with High Touch. Since our members are true professionals, I think any of these would be well received.

Possible topics include:

- Quality Circles.
- Management with Meaning.
- The Corporate Ladder Has a Missing Rung.
- You Ain't There Yet!
- High Tech With High Touch.

Notice how much more readable the second sample is? Even a quick read conveys the message.

Memo Secrets

Eliminate unnecessary closings.

The Closing

Unlike business letters, the best memo closing may be none. Use a closing only when you need to convey a last item of information.

Compare the following closing paragraphs of a memo.

When you have had an opportunity to consider all the options, please give me a call. If you have any questions, please do not hesitate to contact me.

This closing contains no necessary information. It is weakened even more by the vague reference, *please give me a call.* It continues its ineffectiveness by closing with a cliche: *If you have any questions, please do not hesitate to contact me.*

Can this closing be improved? No. It is unnecessary and therefore should not even be written.

Please meet in my office on Tuesday, August 3, at 9:00 A.M. to finalize these plans.

This is an example of a closing paragraph that is effective—written in brief specific language.

PUTTING IT ALL TOGETHER

Now that you have reviewed the basic principles of planning and writing memos, it is time to put your new skill to work. Refer to the preceding pages as often as necessary.

First, prepare a memo plan for the situation described below. Then, write a first draft of the memo. Finally, do any necessary rewriting or editing for a final copy.

> Write a memo to all department managers telling them that the preliminary architectural plans for a building expansion are ready to be reviewed. These plans will be presented by Letitia Villacorta, president of your company, at a meeting on Tuesday of next week in your office. Each manager should bring 12 copies of the respective five-year department plans. This is an exciting meeting because these plans have been in the works for 36 months.

Use the space here and on the next page to prepare your memo-writing plan.

_____

_____

_____

_____

_____

_____

_____

_____

_____

_____

_____

_____

_____

Reminder: Did you sequence the points?

You may wish to prepare the first draft on a separate sheet of paper. Use the space below to draft your final memo.

_____

_____

_____

_____

_____

_____

_____

_____

_____

_____

_____

_____

_____

_____

_____

_____

_____

_____

_____

_____

_____

_____

_____

_____

_____

_____

A sample solution appears on page 89. Look at the important points in the suggested memo. Compare them to those in your memo.

THE ELECTRONIC MESSAGE—
AN INSTANT MEMO

Electronic Message Secrets

Remember there is a human being at the other end of the line.

The use of electronic messages is growing rapidly. It has been estimated that, by the year 2000, 60 billion messages will be sent annually. What do you need to know to use this medium successsfully?

Electronic messages are another form of interoffice memos. Many of the checkpoints from the previous chapter also apply to electronic messages. In addition, the following guidelines will be helpful to you.

Effective Electronic Messages

- The reader cannot see your face; thus, the nuances of communication are missing. Avoid jokes, sarcasm, threats, or any tools of verbal communication that might be misinterpreted.

- Write an attention-getting opening sentence. As more and more messages are sent, yours must stand out if it is to be read.

- Write the main message—and the main message only.

- Limit your message to one screen, if possible.

- Review your message before sending it. Is it grammatically correct? Are all words spelled correctly? Your image and your credibility are on the line.

- Avoid using the system for personal messages. Electronic messages may not be as private as you think.

- Be sure you save or print a copy when you need a record of your message.

Chapter Checkpoints

Memo-Writing Checkpoints

✓ Always begin with a writing plan.

✓ Put the most important information in the first sentence or paragraph.

✓ Tell the reader what you want done as quickly as possible.

✓ Write short, simple sentences.

✓ When appropriate, use a listing to expand or support the main message.

✓ Eliminate all unnecessary information.

✓ Eliminate unnecessary closings.

Memo Protocol

✓ Never write a memo you are unwilling to have other people read.

✓ Never assume that memo information will be kept confidential.

✓ Never ignore the chain of command.

✓ Avoid exaggeration.

✓ Avoid humor; never use sarcasm.

✓ Don't use a memo to criticize another person or department.

✓ If you write a negative memo, delay sending it.

CHAPTER

3 | The Five C's of Good Writing

This chapter will help you to:

- Understand the application of the five C's of good writing to business writing for success.
- Master the application of the five C's on business copy.

Brigitte Svensen, medical office supervisor, composes many explanation letters to patients, referral doctors, and hospital and extended care administrators. The nature of her correspondence has taught her to be careful with details. But she still lacks confidence in her total writing ability. She wonders whether there is a simple set of guidelines that she could use to evaluate her own writing.

Brigitte would find Chapter 3 very helpful. The five C's are universal guidelines to good business writing. If you are careful to observe these in your writing, you will feel your confidence grow as you write better and more successful letters and memos. ■

DEFINING THE FIVE C'S

What are the five C's that are so important to good writing?

As an introduction, each of the five C's (conciseness, completeness, courtesy, clarity, and correctness) are briefly defined here. The following pages will show their applications to business writing.

Conciseness:	Writing the message in as few words as possible.
Completeness:	Ensuring that all information needed by the reader to respond or act is included.
Courtesy:	Showing consideration for the reader.

31

Clarity:	Writing clearly.
Correctness:	Checking the letter or memo for accuracy of all statements and details.

APPLYING THE FIVE C'S

Conciseness

Writing the message in as few words as possible.

Conciseness

Being concise does not always mean being brief. For example, you may write a 20-page report that is concise if it says only what is necessary.

Being concise means avoiding unnecessary explanations. If the added information is not important to the main message, don't include it.

Being concise means avoiding three common writing traps: excess words, redundancies, and long words in place of short ones. Study the examples below of each of these.

Wordiness

First writing:	As much as I would like to meet you for lunch on Thursday, I cannot because my seven-year-old granddaughter, Rochelle, is having her first tap dance recital on that date. I have an 11:00 appointment on Monday, but I think I will be finished in time for lunch. Is your schedule free on that date?
Revision:	I am unable to join you for lunch on Thursday. Could we reschedule for Monday?

Redundancies

First writing:	Past experience tells me that our first priority should be consideration of the final outcome.
Revision:	Experience suggests that our priority should be consideration of the outcome.

3

Long words

First writing: We need to maximize our profits in the coming quarter.

Revision: We need to add to our profits in the next quarter.

Completeness

Ensuring that all information needed by the reader to respond or act is included.

Completeness

Completeness involves presenting all the facts.

- If you ask a person to call, include a phone number.
- If you invite a person to a meeting, give the date, the time, and the place.
- If you expect the reader to take action, present all the facts necessary to do so.
- If you are making a recommendation, provide supporting data.

Study the examples below for a better understanding of completeness.

Missing details

First writing: Please call me when you reach your decision.

Revision: Please call me at 702-225-1990 when you reach your decision.

First writing: Please meet me on Tuesday at 2:00 P.M.

Revision: Please meet me on Tuesday, September 15, at 2:00 P.M. in the Executive Conference Room at Metro Airport.

Missing facts or data

First writing: My department members simply cannot tolerate the continued tardiness of Janet Adams. My recommendation is immediate termination.

Revision: The continued tardiness of Ms. Adams (see below) is having a negative effect on my department members, and I recommend immediate termination.

Janet Adams		Emp. No. 363-89-7878
Verbal warning:	Feb. 1, 1993	
Late 5 min.	Feb. 15, 1993	
Late 7 min.	Feb. 22, 1993	
Late 15 min.	Feb. 23, 1993	
First written warning:	Feb. 28, 1993	
Late 10 min.	Mar. 2, 1993	
Late 15 min.	Mar. 5, 1993	

> ## Courtesy
>
> Showing consideration for the reader.

Courtesy

Courtesy is self-explanatory. It refers to using words such as *please* and *thank you* as often as appropriate.

Courtesy also involves keeping the reader's interests and feelings in mind. The courteous letter uses positive words and phrases rather than negative ones.

Even bad news letters can be courteous and warm. When you are faced with a bad news/good news situation, always deliver the bad news first. Then write the good news, adding emphasis to it by putting it at the end of the sentence.

3

Lack of courtesy

First writing:	Your response to our letter last week arrived today.
Revision:	Thank you for responding so quickly to our letter.

Negative expressions

First writing:	You claimed in your complaint letter . . .
Revision:	You stated in your letter . . .

Bad news/good news

First writing:	I would recommend that you contact Manuel Martinez since I cannot accept your invitation to speak to your group.
Revision:	Since I am unable to accept your invitation to speak to your group, may I suggest that you call Manuel Martinez, who is an excellent speaker.

Clarity

Writing clearly.

Clarity

Clarity involves being specific. A clear letter or memo leaves no doubts in the reader's mind.

Promote clarity in your writing by avoiding vague expressions. Say what you mean. Use a specific noun rather than a general noun preceded by one or two modifiers.

Resist the temptation to use jargon in your writing. Jargon exists in every industry, is understood by insiders, and may be appropriate for in-house communications. However, it is unfamiliar to outsiders and is not appropriate for outside correspondence.

You may find that you can improve the clarity of your writing by controlling the length of your sentences. Generally, aim for 10 to 14 words per sentence.

Vague expression

First writing:	The change in managers will have a major impact on our sales forecasts. (Will the impact be positive or negative?)
Revision:	The change in managers will have a major negative impact on our sales forecasts.

Vague noun

First writing:	The woman bought a new black puppy.
Revision:	Mayor Susan Marx bought a black Doberman puppy.

Jargon

First writing:	We need to interface about the bug in the CPU.
Revision:	We need to talk about the problem with your computer.

Long sentence

First writing:	Hopefully, I will be able to expedite the termination notice to achieve processing no later than the fifteenth of January.
Revision:	I hope to wrap up the termination process by January 15.

Correctness

Checking the letter or memo for accuracy of all statements and details.

Correctness

Remember Smoky Bear's slogan, "Only you can prevent forest fires!"? Only you, the writer, can check for accuracy of statements and details. Another person reading your work may be totally uninformed.

Be particularly careful to proofread numbers, such as dates, times, amounts of money, and so forth.

Make sure the statement says what you intend it to say. Check the usage of similar words, such as *affect/effect* and *less/fewer*. Refer to Chapter 5 for a review of frequently confused words.

Use the spell check feature of your word processor. But remember a spell check does not substitute for a careful reading by the writer.

Inaccuracy of statement

First writing: Every one at the meeting agreed we must proceed with the project.
                   (Did *everyone* agree, or is *a consensus* more accurate? Only you know.)
Revision: A consensus of those present agreed we must proceed with the project.

Inaccuracy in numbers

First writing: We will be closed on Thanksgiving Day, November 25, 1992.
                   (In 1992, Thanksgiving falls on November 26.)
Revision: We will be closed on Thanksgiving Day, November 26, 1992.

Misuse of similar words

First writing: Its only three miles further down the road.
Revision: It's only three miles farther down the road.

Errors overlooked by spell check

First writing:	Margeaux and Petros were to tired to finish there report.
Revision:	Margeaux and Petros were too tired to finish their report.

 R e v i e w   &   P r a c t i c e

You have just learned five basic principles of business writing. You now have an opportunity to apply this learning by improving each of the following sentences. On the line provided, rewrite each sentence.

Conciseness

It has come to my attention that our employees, new and old, have developed a habit of taking extended coffee and lunch breaks.

_____

_____

Completeness

Your performance review will be next Tuesday morning.

_____

Courtesy

Your failure to send in your monthly payment upsets me.

_____

Clarity

A comprehensive review of your in-house substance abuse program will be conducted by members of the local university's Wellness Division.

_____

_____

Correctness

Four months have only 30 days: April, June, September, and October.

_____

Sample solutions appear on page 89.

SAMPLE LETTERS

First writing

Note lack of:

Conciseness/
Clarity————————

Completeness————————

Correctness————————

Courtesy————————

GRO-RITE LANDSCAPING

P.O. BOX 375   Las Vegas, NV 89117

_____

June 23, 199—

Star Nurseries
3500 Cheyenne Ave.
Henderson, NV 89015

Ladies/Gentlemen

• It has come to my attention that the fiscus auriculata you have supplied to us in recent weeks have been very inferior to those you normally supply. In fact, the last three or four shipments have been noticeably poor.

• Everyone knows that these plants grow well in our area, and problems simply do not occur.

• I expect you to take care of this matter immediately.

Sincerely

Gary Rodeghier
President

pr

Revised Writing

Note use of:

Conciseness

Clarity

Completeness

Correctness

Courtesy

GRO-RITE LANDSCAPING

P.O. BOX 375   Las Vegas, NV 89117

_____

June 23, 199—

Star Nurseries
3500 Cheyenne Ave.
Henderson, NV 89015

Ladies/Gentlemen

Our orders of June 2, 15, and 20 each included 8 ficus trees (5'). The trees shipped to us were not of your usual high quality. We anticipate needing to replace some of these for our customers.

Since ficus trees normally do well in our area, our initial assumption is that the problem lies with the grower. Would you please look into this matter and call me at 702-225-1900 as soon as you have some information.

Sincerely

Gary Rodeghier
President

pr

CHAPTER REVIEW: PUTTING IT ALL TOGETHER

You are now ready to put it all together and apply the five C's of business writing to a sample letter.

Look at the text of the letter below. A quick reading will convince you that the writer either is unaware of the principles of writing or chooses to ignore them. You may find it helpful to review the five C's. You may wish to highlight specific instances where one of the principles should have been applied.

3

February 1, 199—

Martin G. LeFavre
3301 Eastern Ave., Apt. 211
Wichita, KS 67215

Dear Martha

Your letter of application for an entry-level sales position in our company has been added to our file of active applicants. We do not have any openings at this time.

This file remains open for a period of six months. If you wish to be considered after that time, you must submit a new application. Sometimes when we have a particular interest in a person of your qualifications, we will move your application into the new active file. It also helps if you submit to a particular person rather than to the human resources department.

Good Luck in your job search!

Sincerely

First rewrite the letter in the space provided on the next page.

After you have written your letter, review it carefully for conciseness, completeness, courtesy, clarity, and correctness. Can you identify specific examples of each of the five C's?

A sample solution appears on page 90.

3

4 | The Writer's Edge

This chapter will help you to:

- Recognize common writing practices that diminish the effect of your correspondence.
- Prepare superior letters and memos through applying principles to write for results.

Margareta Gurrieri, a paralegal, took time one day to read some letters she had written. To her dismay, she found that she had fallen into some poor writing habits: She wrote wordy sentences, used jargon frequently, and talked down to the clients. She recognized sentences that would have been more emphatic with the simple use of an active verb. She knew that she needed to brush up her writing skills.

Chapter 4 is designed to help experienced writers like Margareta, as well as novice writers, recognize when to use the write-for-results principles. ■

PRINCIPLE 1: USE AS FEW WORDS AS POSSIBLE

A recent college graduate began her resume with the following career objective:

OBJECTIVE
To be in a position to utilize my excellent educational preparation, my meaningful work experience, and my outstanding people skills in a middle management position that will give me a good opportunity to grow professionally and personally in very important ways.

Does this statement impress you? Probably not. Would you think "Just tell me what your objective is!" The fewer words you use, the more powerful your message is.

Excessive words can creep into your writing easily. Check the list on the left below. Do any of these appear in your writing?

4

Excessive wording	Improved wording
at a later date	later or then
at all times	always
at this point in time	now
can be in a position to	can
due to the fact that	because
each and every one	every one
firstly, secondly, thirdly,	first, second, third
in compliance with your request	at your request
in the event of	if
in the majority of instances	usually
inasmuch as	since
on a monthly basis	monthly
owing to the fact that	since
_____	_____
_____	_____
_____	_____
_____	_____
_____	_____

Can you think of wordy expressions you use? Add to the list above.

PRINCIPLE 2: NEVER USE TWO WORDS WHEN ONE WILL DO

Most of us say more than is necessary to make our point. We carry this habit over into writing. Redundant expressions are another form of excessive wording. Some redundant expressions have become cliches. For that reason, you may not even recognize them as redundant.

Can you identify the redundancies in the following sentence?

The consensus of opinion is that our advance planning was absolutely essential.

Did you spot *consensus* of opinion, *advance* planning, *absolutely* essential? Look over the following list of other common redundant expressions. Note that each of the italicized words is unnecessary.

actual experience	*final* conclusion
and *etc.*	first *and foremost*
ask *the question*	following *after*
attached *hereto*	for *a period of* two weeks
at some later *date*	*foreign* imports
basic fundamentals	*free* gratis
blend/join/merge/mix *together*	goals *and objectives*
circle *around*	*group* meeting
close proximity/scrutiny	large/small *in size*
collect/combine *together*	*mutual* cooperation
completely filled	*new* innovation
consequent results	*one and* the same
continue *on*	*past* experience
cooperate *together*	plan *ahead/for the future/in advance*
disappear *from sight*	
enclosed *herewith*	reason *is because*
estimated *to be about*	recur/repeat *again*
exact opposites	same *identical*
few *in number*	*true* facts

Underline any of the above expressions that you use. This will increase your awareness of the phrase and help you eliminate it from your writing.

PRINCIPLE 3: USE POSITIVE WORDS AND PHRASES

Do you remember the popular song of the 1940s: "Accentuate the Positive!"? Perhaps the composer was also a writer of business letters because the advice is excellent. Compare the two sentences below.

Negative statement

You overlooked the fact that you failed to make last month's payment.

Positive statement

Were you aware that you did not mail last month's payment?

Which statement is more likely to elicit a positive response from the customer? Which one would you respond to?

Negative expressions can be either direct or implied. If a sentence reads, "You are not qualified for the position," it is a direct negative. If the same sentence reads, "You need more experience to qualify for this position," it is negative by implication. Your task as a writer is to convey negative information in positive language.

Remember, your ultimate goal is to bring about a positive response or action from the reader. You accomplish this more quickly if you do not scold or make the reader feel guilty.

Two pointers may help you create positive statements for negative situations.

- Avoid beginning a sentence with *you*. You will find that you write a softer sentence when the *you* is placed within the sentence. *Did you understand my point?* is much softer than *You failed to understand my point.*
- Substitute *when* for *if. When you complete your work, we will process your salary increase* implies confidence in the reader more than *If you complete your work, we will process your salary increase.*

PRINCIPLE 4: AVOID CLICHES AND USE JARGON ONLY WHEN APPROPRIATE

Cliches are fad phrases and trite expressions. Americans are experts at creating fad phrases. Initially these can be very effective. With overuse they quickly lose their punch. An example is *user friendly*, a term that came to us in the early 1980s with PCs. It has long since lost its impact.

Many business writers use far too many trite phrases. Your letters and memos should represent your personal expression rather than stilted tradition. Give your correspondence a fresh face; aim for a warm, conversational tone.

There are thousands of cliches in our language. A few of the familiar ones in business usage are listed here. Be aware of cliches in your own writing and eliminate them.

ballpark figure	hands on
bottom line	input
brainstorm	maximize
cost-effective	meaningful
dialogue	prioritize
enclosed herewith	state of the art
first and foremost	thank you in advance

Jargon is insider talk—words and phrases understood by persons in a particular profession or industry. Jargon is a necessary part of communication between persons in the profession but is inappropriate when writing to persons outside your industry who may be unfamiliar with them. As we saw in Chapter 3, jargon interferes with clarity. Samples of jargon taken from several professions would include:

cash cow	feasibility study
CPU	interface
debug	K
DTP	needs assessment
extended family	normative sample
facilitator	quality circles

As you identify jargon in your communications, be sure you observe the following guidelines.

- Limit the use of jargon to those readers who understand it.
- If you must use jargon, include its meaning the first time you use it.

PRINCIPLE 5: BE AWARE OF SEXISM

Good business writers are careful to eliminate all sexist language or infer-ences from their writing. In the past, sexism has been evident in two forms:

> The use of sexist designations: mailman or stewardess.

> The use of sexist pronoun references: the doctor and *his* patients, the nurse and *her* patients.

Sexism in writing can be eliminated in three ways:

- Using *his/her* in place of a single *his* or *her:* Each employee must prepare his/her own report. Note: Many writers consider this an awk-ward construction and avoid it whenever possible.

- Changing the noun to a plural form and using *their:* All employees must prepare their own reports.

- Rewriting the sentence to avoid the use of a pronoun: Reports must be prepared by individual students.

Eliminating sexism from your writing does not mean that you accept a certain political system or philosophy. It simply means that you acknowl-edge the equality of roles that exist in business today. Listed below are samples of gender-specific terms that have changed in recent years.

Original phrase	Improved phrase
chairman	chair, chairperson
fireman	firefighter
housewife	homemaker
man hours	work hours
my girl	my secretary/assistant/support person
policeman	police officer
salesman	salesperson
stewardess	flight attendant
workman	worker/employee

▎ R e v i e w & P r a c t i c e

Apply the five write-for-results principles you have just reviewed to these sample sentences. Rewrite the following sentences to illustrate:

Use as Few Words as Possible

Pursuant to your personal letter of May 15, 199–, we wish to inform you that the aggregate amount of your purchases leaves an account balance of $259.95.

_____

_____

_____

Eliminating Redundant Expressions

It is my personal opinion that the statement attached hereto contains the true facts in the case.

_____

_____

_____

Using Positive Words and Phrases

If you will take time to read the enclosed brochure, you will understand why we demand prompt payment of all accounts.

_____

_____

_____

Eliminating Cliches and Jargon

Thank you in advance for helping us prioritize our needs.

_____

_____

Avoiding Sexist References

The future of each employee lies in his own hands.

_____

_____

Note: Sample solutions are on page 90.

PRINCIPLE 6: USE THE ACTIVE VOICE

Perhaps you will remember the classic definition: Active verbs act; passive verbs are acted upon.

Active verb

Our Roanoke branch *tests* all new products.

Passive verb

All new products are *tested* at our Roanoke branch.

Using active verbs adds power to your writing: Active verbs are more dynamic than passive verbs. Active verbs move your reader to action. Active verbs result in shorter sentences.

Passive verbs can be identified by the presence of a linking verb (is, are, am, was, or were). Compare the two forms below.

Active verb	**Passive verb**
communicated	are communicated
analyzed	were analyzed
thought	was thought

Passive verbs in sentences can usually be converted to active by rewriting the sentence. When you rewrite, be careful that you do not change the meaning.

Passive:	The new policy was recommended by Gerard.
Active:	Gerard recommended the new budget.
Passive:	It has been decided to cancel the program.
Active:	The Executive Committee cancelled the program.

Use the passive voice when the subject of the sentence or the doer of the action is more important than the action.

Appropriate use of passive voice

Minimum standards will be established for all new employees.

(The standards are more important than the employees.)

The worker was seriously injured by the falling beam.

(The worker is more important than the beam.)

PRINCIPLE 7: WRITE *TO* AND NOT DOWN TO YOUR READER

The use of condescending words and phrases in your writing is a more abstract concept than some of the writing principles discussed previously. Condescending expressions are a matter of tone rather than specific words. The same words can be acceptable in one situation and unacceptable (condescending) in another. Condescending is talking down to the reader. The reader senses a scolding or an "I told you so" attitude.

A condescending tone is most apt to creep into your writing when you are displeased with the reader, the reader's action, or lack of the reader's action.

Condescending:	As you are well aware, our policy is to satisfy our customers.
Improved:	As a valued customer, your satisfaction is our goal.

Notice that the first sentence is me-oriented and thus condescending. The second sentence is you-oriented. Which one evokes a positive response from you?

Unfortunately, some writers use a condescending tone to boost their own egos or to express their own sense of self-importance. A common way of doing this is through the use of jargon (see principle 4).

Condescending:	The documentation for your LAN will answer all your questions. If you don't understand the instructions, call our technical support system.
Improved:	You will find the manual for your network very helpful. If you have additional questions, our support staff at 1-800-225-8989 is eager to help you.

If you had recently installed a computer network, which sentence would you find user friendly?

Hints ───────────────────────────────

Every business writer has moments of anger or exasperation. If you can, avoid writing during those times. If you must write, put the letter or memo aside. Read it later and alter the tone before sending it.

PRINCIPLE 8: BIG WORDS ARE UNNECESSARY

Do you want to write power-packed messages? Use short, plain words. Too often the only person you impress with big words is yourself.

Your writing should be appropriate for your audience. Think of the people you most often write to: customers, clients, and colleagues. All these people would rather do business with a warm, helpful human being than a cold, robotlike individual.

What about your superiors? Many executives will tell you that they respond to clear, plain, short messages. They do not have time to interpret your impressive use of the language.

Stilted language:	The cessation of the policy will occur at 12:01 A.M., July 15.
Improved language:	The policy expires at 12:01 A.M., July 15.
Too many big words:	You should proceed to investigate the findings of the study.
Improved language:	Continue your study of the findings.

How can you develop the good writing habit of simple language?

- Write the message naturally, including any big words that come to you.
- Reread the message. Did you write to impress rather than to express?
- Ask yourself: What am I really trying to say?
- Rewrite the message.
- Write down any big words you use unnecessarily. Remember, awareness is the first step to improvement.

Hints ────────────────────────────────

> Have you ever heard a reader complain that a letter or memo was
> too easy to understand?

 Review & Practice

The three writing principles you have just reviewed focused on enhancing
your writing skill. Let's apply this skill to sample sentences. Rewrite the following sentences to illustrate:

Using Active Verbs

The new vacation policy was approved by the employee task force
and will give employees of five years or more an added week of
vacation.

_____

_____

Avoiding a Condescending Tone

Since we have done business for many years, you should know that we
require payment upon delivery, unless prior arrangements have
been made.

_____

_____

Using Simple Words

Enclosed herewith is a copy of the recently passed legislative act
empowering Kansas City homeowners to appeal the tax rates established for their properties.

_____

_____

Note: Suggested sample solutions are on pages 90-91.

PRINCIPLE 9: WRITE DIRECTLY TO THE
INTERESTS OF THE READER

Not considering the interests of your reader could be the reason behind
the other nine writing traps. If you consciously consider the interests of
your reader, you are apt to observe good writing principles. How can you
do this?

4

Visualize your reader. Imagine you and your reader are in the same room holding a conversation. What level of language would you use? What tone would you convey to maintain a positive discussion? What information would you give that person? What response would you expect? All these questions represent issues you want to keep in mind when writing, guaranteeing that you think of your reader first.

Business writing books have called this approach the you attitude. It emphasizes *you* instead of *I/we/me/us*. Consider the following sentences:

I/me attitude	You attitude
If we do not receive your check immediately, we will be unable to continue shipping your orders without prepayment.	You have always enjoyed immediate shipping status. You can retain this convenient rating by sending us your check immediately.
While I remember with pleasure my appearance last year at your awards banquet, I am not available on July 30 this year to speak to your group.	What a pleasure it was to speak to your group last year. I sincerely wish I could join you again this year but, unfortunately, I have another engagement.

Hints ───────────────────────

When you are the reader, what letter tone elicits a favorable response? In other words, if you were the reader, how would you react to the letter you just wrote?

PRINCIPLE 10: ARE THE DETAILS CORRECT?

A local dental office routinely sends letters to new patients. The letters are concise, warm, and personal. The message is lost due to poor formatting, typos, two typefaces, and two typestyles. It is obviously a form letter, mass-produced on a poor copier.

When the letter is brought to the attention of Jodie Menendez, the dental office manager, she says that it is out of her control because the letter is prepared by a service.

Jodie is responsible. If she has hired a secretarial service, she has a right to expect quality work. The image of the secretarial service is not affected, but the image of the dental practice is tarnished. ■

Do you think your job is done when you finish writing a letter? Composing the letter is only the first step.

As the writer, you are also responsible for error-free copy, accurate information or details, and appropriate formatting. If you send your letters to a support person for typing, you hope that person will also assume some responsibility for the accuracy of the contents. However, when you sign the letter, you are implying approval of the contents and the appearance. Do you take pride in the letters bearing your signature? Are you reasonably certain of their accuracy?

The quality of your correspondence is a reflection of you. What image are you projecting?

- Scan your correspondence before signing it. Does it appear balanced on the page? Is there enough white space to encourage reading?
- Read the letter for content. Does it say what you intend to say? Is the tone positive?
- Read the letter for accuracy. Are the spelling and grammar correct? Are names, dates, and other details correct?

■ Review & Practice

You have just completed the review of the final two write-for-results principles: considering the interests of the reader and paying attention to details. Both of these represent important refinements in your writing.

Read the sentences below. Write an improved sentence for each one.

Considering the Interests of the Reader

We are unable to fill your order for one file cabinet because you failed to specify the color or size.

_____

_____

_____

Paying Attention to Details

Each of the divisions have made a firm commitment to better quality control.

_____

_____

_____

Sample solutions are on page 91.

CHAPTER REVIEW: PUTTING IT ALL TOGETHER

Now that you are aware of the 10 write-for-results principles of business writing, you are ready to apply them in your writing.

Read the letter below. Remembering the 10 write-for-results principles, can you spot them in this letter? Highlight them for review. Refer to the previous pages as needed.

February 20, 199—

Ara Godosian, Manager
ABC Suppliers Inc.
P.O. Box 4857
Newark, NJ 07152

Dear Mr. Godosian

Due to the fact that, in the majority of recent instances, your account with us has had an overdue past balance, we can no longer sell merchandise to you on a cash basis.

We are sorry to take this unfortunate action, but you have been warned on previous occasions that it might be necessary.

I must ask the question: What is the problem? Is your manager of accounts payable unable to keep his accounts in order? We are sorry, but we have to pay our bills too. The bottom line is continuing to carry your account is no longer cost-effective for us.

Lastly, since my personal experience is working with you has always been positive, I have asked that your account be held in our active files for a period of 10 days. If you wish to respond to this action, you will need to do so within that time frame.

Sincerely

Patrick Monaghan
Controller

Rewrite the letter in the space provided here.

As you're writing, think about the writing principles. Are there particular ones that you never applied in your writing? After you've rewritten the letter, review it closely. Have you applied each of the 10 writing principles?

A sample solution appears on page 91.

4

5 | Using the Right Word

This chapter will help you to:

- Feel confident that every word is spelled correctly.
- Recognize the most frequently misspelled words in business writing.
- Use correct grammar, recognizing the five areas where errors are most likely to occur:

  Change in tenses.

  Agreement of subject and verb.

  Agreement of pronoun and antecedent.

  Dangling modifiers.

  Possessives.

FREQUENTLY MISSPELLED WORDS

Did you know that many of the spelling errors that appear in business writing occur within the same words?

Knowing these words and their trouble spots can help you eliminate potential spelling errors from your writing. Listed here are 25 of the most frequently misspelled words. Do you recognize any words that cause you problems? Circle those words.

accommodate	achievement	acknowledgment
analysis	benefited	calendar
commitment	convenient	criticism
description	develop	embarrass
extension	judgment	loose
occurrence	possession	precede

5

privilege   proceed   recommend

separate   similar   supersede

surprise

Hints

The key to improving your own spelling is to know what words you
tend to misspell. When you identify the word, isolate the trouble spot.

The spelling problems in these words tend to be the same for most people. Look at the list below. The trouble spot in each word is underlined. Note especially the trouble spot in the words that you circled.

accommodate	achievement	acknowledgment
analysis	benefited	calendar
commitment	convenient	criticism
description	develop	embarrass
extension	judgment	loose
occurrence	possession	precede
privilege	proceed	recommend
separate	similar	supersede
surprise		

FREQUENTLY CONFUSED WORDS

Many similar words in our language cause even the most careful writer to pause. For example, when do you use *accept* or *except,* or *to, too,* or *two*? Being able to distinguish between these similar words ensures the accuracy of your writing.

Since the spell checker on your word processor will not highlight these words, it is very important for you to know how each one is used.

Review the following list of frequently confused words. Review the word, its definition, and its use in a sentence.

Accept, Except:
Accept means to receive something; except means to exclude.

I cannot accept your explanation.	Everyone except the patient was pleased.

Affect, Effect:
Affect means to influence; effect (as a noun) means a result; effect (as a verb) means to bring about.

Will the change affect your plans?	The effects were immediately noticeable.
How can we effect this change in policy?	

All Ready, Already:

All ready means completely prepared; already means previously.
Are you all ready for your presentation?   It's already lunch time.

All Right, Alright:

All right means satisfactory; alright is nonstandard English and should be avoided.
The schedule is all right with me.

Beside, Besides:

Beside means next to; besides means in addition to.

The printer is beside the desk.   Besides Mr. Klein, who is not coming?

Capital, Capitol:

Capital refers to money or the seat of state government; capitol refers to the building in which a legislative body meets.

How much capital will you need?   The citizens visited the capitol.

Ensure, Insure:

Ensure means to assure; insure means to protect against loss.

The added step will ensure success.   Is your automobile adequately insured?

Farther, Further:

Farther refers to physical distance; further means additional. (In informal usage, these are often used interchangeably.)

Reno is farther west than Denver.   Do you need further information?

Few, Less:

Fewer refers to number; less refers to degree.

Fewer than 10 responded.   It occurred less than six months ago.

Principal, Principle:

Principal means main or first in importance or the head of a school; principle means rule.

The principal cause was unemployment.   It's a matter of principle.

The principal commended the fine teacher.

Some Time, Sometime, Sometimes:

Some time means a period of time; sometime means a vague, unspecified time; sometimes means occasionally.

I will need some time to do my work.   I plan to revisit Russia sometime.

Sometimes I wish I were young again.

Than, Then:

Than means compared to; then means at that time.

Let's meet today rather than next week.   I plan to visit the project then.

■ R e v i e w   &   P r a c t i c e

Practice using some of these frequently confused words by completing the sentences.

Capital/Capitol	What is the _____ of Pennsylvania?
Principal/Principle	Marietta was recently promoted to _____ of the school.
Some Time/Sometime/ Sometimes	_____ we forget that it requires _____ to learn to use new software.
Fewer/Less	Would we have _____ problems if we had _____ employees?
Affect(s)/Effect(s)	The _____ of the devastating hurricane will _____ hundreds of residents for many years.
Ensure/Insure	Our goal is to _____ the success of the project.
Than/Then	If you had been given a choice _____, would you have chosen to relocate rather _____ to stay?
Farther/Further	How much _____ do we have to drive?
Accept/Except	I simply cannot _____ the job offer at that salary.
All Ready/Already	We are _____ past our deadline. Are you _____ to defend our position?

Solutions are on page 92.

USING CORRECT GRAMMAR

Like common spelling errors, grammatical errors in business writing often occur in one of four categories:

1. Change in tenses.
2. Agreement of subject and verb.
3. Agreement of pronouns and their antecedents.
4. Possessives.

Understanding each of these and watching for them in your own writing will go a long way toward establishing your reputation as a careful writer.

Change in Tenses

Even the mention of *tense* strikes fear in many writers, perhaps including yourself. You may recall a former English teacher speaking a language you never understood: past, present, and future tense; past, present, and future participles; and even perfect tenses.

This discussion will eliminate the jargon of tense usage and help you spot the most obvious misuse of tense in your own writing. Let's look at some examples.

Shift in verb tense

First writing: We were balancing our books. Suddenly the lights go out.

Revision: We were balancing our books. Suddenly the lights went out.

The verbs in the first writing shift from the past to the present. Both verbs in the revised sentence are in the past.

Shift in voice

First writing: You need to be aware of potential errors that keep our work from being acceptable.

Revision: You need to be aware of potential errors that keep your work from being acceptable.

                   We need to be aware of potential errors that keep our work from being acceptable.

In the first writing, the voice shifts from the second person (you) to the third person (our). Two revisions are shown; the better one is the one that conveys the intended meaning.

Agreement of Subject and Verb

You must remember one simple guideline:

THE SUBJECT AND VERB MUST AGREE IN NUMBER.

If you use a singular subject, use a singular verb.
If you use a plural subject, use a plural verb.

Lack of agreement

First writing: Each one are eligible for the award.

Revision: Each one is eligible for the award.

Your errors in agreement are not apt to be that obvious. The following pointers will help you refine your skill in agreement.

- When intervening words appear between the subject and the verb, identify the simple subject.

  Each one *of the employees* is eligible for the award.

  One is the simple, singular subject; therefore, the correct verb is the singular *is.*

- *There* or *here* is never the subject of the sentence. Find the simple subject elsewhere in the sentence and select the verb that agrees with it.

There were 70 retirees at the annual luncheon.

The simple, plural subject is *retirees*; the plural *were* agrees with it.

- *Each, every, many a*, and the indefinite pronouns take singular verbs.

  Many a young man wishes he had studied harder.
  Everybody thrives on compliments.

  The singular verbs *wishes* and *thrives* agree with the singular subjects.

- When subjects are joined by *either/or* or *neither/nor*, the verb agrees with the subject closer to it.

  Neither the president nor his assistants agree with the new policy.

  Assistants is nearer the plural *agree*.

Agreement of Pronouns and their Antecedents

You also must remember one rule about the agreement of pronouns and antecedents:

PRONOUNS MUST AGREE WITH THEIR ANTECEDENTS.

The antecedent is simply the word for which the pronoun stands.

The technician forgot one of her important tools.

Her is the pronoun; *technician* is the antecedent.

Agreement of pronouns and antecedents must occur in two contexts:

- Agreement in number. Choose a singular pronoun for a singular antecedent; choose a plural pronoun for a plural antecedent.
- Agreement in gender. When the antecedent is specifically male or female, make sure the pronoun agrees with it. As is often the case, the antecedent could refer to either or both sexes. Sexist references are unacceptable in today's business environment. The examples below will help you avoid this.

Lack of agreement in number

First writing:	Every one of the young women forgot their sales manuals.
Revision:	Every one of the young women forgot her sales manuals.
First writing:	Neither partner, Christina nor Josephine, wishes to give up their personal secretary.
Revision:	Neither partner, Christina nor Josephine, wishes to give up her personal secretary.

Lack of agreement in gender

First writing:	Each instructor will write his own evaluation.
Revision:	Each instructor will write his/her own evaluation.
Preferred revision:	All instructors will write their own evaluation.

Rewriting the sentence is often the best way to eliminate sexism.

Possessives

An easy-to-remember rule will help you form possessives correctly:

If the word does not end in s, add 's. If the word already ends in s, add the apostrophe.

Words not ending in *s*

Base word	Possessive form
employer	employer's
assistant	assistant's
director	director's
women	women's
day	day's

Words ending in *s*

Base word	Possessive form
typists	typists'
ladies	ladies'
managers	managers'
girls	girls'
weeks	weeks'

Also consider the following when forming possessives.

- When the base word ends in *s,* add *'s* when you pronounce the additional syllable. Add only the apostrophe if you do not pronounce the added syllable.

  the actress's costume   Sears' warehouse

  Gladys's new house   Ms. James' assistants

- Some terms are descriptive terms rather than possessives. Do not add an apostrophe to these.

  the Word Processors Consortium   United States budget

  American Bankers Association   Massachusetts laws

■ Review & Practice

You have completed a quick review of four of the language elements that need to be considered by the business writer. You can now apply what you have learned to the following sentences. Read each sentence and correct as appropriate. Correct a word or phrase, or rewrite the sentence, as appropriate.

Change in Tense

The staff meeting began sharply at 9 A.M.; at 9:45 Concetta strolls in.

5

Agreement of Subject and Verb

Neither the controller nor the analyst want to change the current system.

Agreement of Pronoun and Antecedent

The surgeon must be dedicated to his task.

Possessives

When will your boss' monthly sales report be ready?

Sample solutions are on page 92.

CHAPTER REVIEW: PUTTING IT ALL TOGETHER

You have just reviewed the finishing touches that create successful business documents—documents that bring results. You are now ready to apply this knowledge to a sample letter.

Read the following letter. The contents of the letter are basically good. However, its effectiveness is lost in little errors. Correct them, referring to the preceding pages as necessary.

August 17, 199—

Marty Levitz, Managing Director
Showtime Theatricals
4556 East 56th Street
New York, NY 09056

Dear Marty

Thanks for confirming our commitment to participate in the December Festival of Lights. Each of our principle performers are already to studying their roles. Your enthusiasm has captured us, to!

Its such an exciting time here. It is our priviledge to be a sponsor of the Physically Challenged Children's Day events at Hyde Park on September 15. I recall that you have had a keen interest in this in the passed. Julie was speaking at our planning session last Thursday when the lights go out. Never a dull moment—or a blank calender!

Everyone sends his regards. I'll be in touch very soon.

Sincerely

Esther Rabinowitz
Scheduling Director

jek

5

Rewrite the letter in the space provided. A sample solution appears on page 93.

_____

_____

_____

_____

_____

_____

_____

_____

_____

_____

_____

_____

_____

_____

_____

_____

_____

_____

_____

_____

_____

_____

_____

_____

_____

_____

_____

_____

_____

_____

_____

_____

Post-Test

Congratulations! You have just taken another important step in your professional development by completing *Writing for Business Results*.

This post-test is provided as a quick means of reinforcing the material you have just covered.

Approximate time to complete: 15 minutes

INSTRUCTIONS: Circle the letter of the correct answer.

1. Which of the following are good reasons for writing a business letter?
    a. To avoid conveying embarrassing information by phone.
    b. To respond to an inquiry.
    c. To prove one's worth to the employer by generating paperwork.
    d. To avoid a personal contact.

2. If you have difficulty getting started when writing, the best solution is to:
    a. Prepare a draft copy.
    b. Put it off until the end of the day after your other work is done.
    c. Begin writing.
    d. Write a final copy on your first try to make up for lost time.

3. The beginning of the letter is important because:
    a. It identifies you as the writer.
    b. Dull openings are seldom recouped later.
    c. You have four seconds to gain your reader's attention.
    d. Most people never read the last part of the letter.

4. The proper sequence for writing a letter or memo is:
    a. Plan, arrange, fill in details, and write.
    b. Plan and write.

    c. Gather details, make a plan, and write.

    d. Write individual paragraphs, arrange them in proper sequence, and rewrite.

5. Which of the following closings would be most appropriate for a sales letter?

    a. You are a phone call away from enjoying your new widget!

    b. If you want to order a widget, please call me.

    c. Widgets cost only $9.95 each.

    d. We hope you will seriously consider purchasing a widget soon.

6. The readability quotient of your letter involves:

    a. The reading level.

    b. The amount of friendliness that emanates from your writing.

    c. The overall appearance of your letter.

    d. The number of paragraphs you have used.

7. The most critical question you can ask yourself before writing is:

    a. Whom am I writing to?

    b. What do I want the reader to know or do after reading this letter/memo?

    c. Who else might read this?

    d. When should I write?

8. One of the secrets of successful memos is:

    a. Say only what is necessary.

    b. Keep the length to two or three paragraphs.

    c. Write as often as necessary until you are certain the message is understood.

    d. Write a friendly last paragraph.

9. Electronic messages differ from memos in which of the following ways?

    a. Since they are transmitted via computer, their importance is understood.

b. The language of electronic messages is more succinct.

c. It is never necessary to keep a hard copy.

d. They are more personal.

10. Conciseness, one of the five C's of business writing, is:

a. Using long words and repeating words as necessary.

b. Writing as briefly as possible.

c. Eliminating excess and long words, as well as redundant expressions.

d. Presenting all the facts.

11. You can achieve clarity in your writing by:

a. Using jargon, so the reader understands your position.

b. Controlling the number of paragraphs.

c. Avoiding the use of vague language and jargon.

d. Writing very short sentences.

12. Which of the following sentences applies the write-for-results principles?

a. At a later date we will review our position.

b. Thank you in advance for your cooperation.

c. We are certain you can never understand our position.

d. Your concerns are our concerns.

13. A condescending tone in writing is:

a. Sometimes necessary in order to convey the message.

b. A matter of tone rather than words.

c. Writing at an elementary reading level.

d. Avoiding the use of big words.

14. Which of the following sentences is grammatically correct?

a. Neither person, Mary or Juan, wishes to give up his secretary.

b. Every one of the members is planning to participate.

c. The three manager's offices are being renovated.

d. There is a number of people who have not responded.

15. Which of the following sentences contains no spelling errors?

    a. The controller said the major capitol committment was a positive step.

    b. Melinda Jones will supercede Richard Cruz next month.

    c. We are unable to accomodate your request at this time.

    d. Your recommendation is accepted.

ANSWERS

1. b	2. c	3. b	4. a	5. a
6. a	7. a	8. a	9. b	10. c
11. c	12. a	13. b	14. b	15. d

Sample Letters

The sample letters shown on the following pages were all created in block format style, but they could also be correctly presented in modified block format style. Refer back to Chapter 1, Letters, on pages 12-13 to review both styles.

ADJUSTMENT LETTER

May 15, 199—

Sylvia Jordan, Manager
Madison Business Suppliers
P.O. Box 1221
Silver Spring, MD 20923

Dear Ms. Jordan

On February 28, 199—, you installed a water purification system in our office building. On the following dates we requested service: March 3, 10, 20, 25; April 7, 14, 20, 23; May 2, 9, and 10. Once again, the system is not functioning today.

We feel that we have been more than patient with the system and the work of your technicians. As I said on the phone this morning, I want this system removed immediately. Also, please issue a check for $935.35, the amount we have paid to date.

Please complete the above actions no later than May 22, 199—.

Sincerely

Peter J. Pososki
President

jt

- Provide details of the original purchase or service.
- State the complaint clearly and concisely.
- State the action you wish the reader to take.

APPOINTMENT LETTER

May 15, 199—

Dante Cantemessa
8901 Birch Avenue – Apt. 225
Bennington, VT 05221

Dear Mr. Cantemessa

Sadie Tomkins, primary interviewer for regional staff positions, has reviewed your application. Ms. Tomkins would like to interview you on Monday, June 3, 199—, at 9 A.M. in the Berkshire Room of the Bennington Lodge.

Please bring complete names and addresses of your references with you. If you have any other credentials that you feel might be helpful, bring them also.

Please confirm this appointment by calling 617-778-8080 no later than Monday, May 26.

Sincerely

Michael Capizzio
Administrative Assistant

kl

- Give specific details of date, time, and place of appointment.
- Add any special information.
- Give specific information for confirming appointment.

APPRECIATION LETTER

May 15, 199—

Seiji Esawa, M.D.
Bayside Medical Clinic #105
565 Rancho Drive
San Mateo, CA 94489

Dear Dr. Esawa

Thank you for the inspiring talk you gave to our students at their annual awards banquet. Several of the students expressed sincere appreciation for your "renewing their dreams."

When I asked you to speak, I recalled a similar presentation you made to a group of practitioners at San Rafael some months ago. I knew you were the ideal person to challenge our students.

Best wishes for your continued success.

Sincerely

Hattie Canty
Placement Director

fv

- Express appreciation, citing occasion.
- When appropriate, add a personal note.
- Close with a statement of good wishes.

COLLECTION LETTER

May 15, 199—

Jose Vidal
3209 Oak Avenue
La Crosse, IN 46348

Dear Mr. Vidal

Our quarterly review of accounts reveals that your account is now two months past due. Your many years as a good customer suggest that this is very unusual.

Are our records correct? Are there extenuating circumstances that we should know about in order to work out a payment plan? Of course, if you have mailed your check and we simply have not received it, we need to know that immediately.

Would you please use the enclosed envelope to send us your check for $185.23 or an explanation of this matter.

Sincerely

Helena Eggert-Rojas
Accounts Payable Secretary

mn

- State the problem.
- Express concern, particularly if this is the first letter.
- State action desired.

INQUIRY LETTER

May 15, 199—

Time Distributors
P.O. Box 355
Staten Island, NY 10325

Ladies and Gentlemen

Our publishing company is planning its annual sales meeting on June 30, 199—, in Atlanta, Georgia. Approximately 225 persons will attend.

While I realize the time is short, is it possible to obtain 250 copies of your brochure "Quality Time in Quality Lives" before June 15? These can be shipped C.O.D. to my attention at the above address.

If possible, would you call my assistant, Ivan Jacobs, at 401-885-3453, within the next week to let him know whether or not these are available. Your cooperation is very much appreciated.

Sincerely

Kazam Soroosh
Employment Relations

vc

- State purpose of letter by providing necessary background information.
- Make request.
- Provide all important details.
- Express appreciation or request response.

ORDER LETTER

May 15, 199—

Quick Copy Suppliers
P.O. Box 667
Madison, WI 53710

Ladies/Gentlemen

Please send the following items to the above address via Fast Express Next Day Air:

Quantity	Catalog No.	Item	Unit Price	Total
15	675-XS	Cartridge Toner 25	105.25	1578.75
15 cases	2323-Q	Card Stock—Canary	45.10	676.50

Our purchase order No. 6675 is enclosed. Thank you.

Sincerely

Andrew Kim
Warehouse Inventory Specialist

bbn

- Give specific ordering information—make sure all information about the item is included.
- Tell how payment is to be made.
- Give shipping information.

REGRETS LETTER

May 15, 199—

Avran Hamani, Program Director
Greater Omaha Small Business Association
9090 Menominee Street
Omaha, NE 68125

Dear Avran

Christine Blews has asked me to express her deep regrets that she is unable to accept your invitation to speak at the July meeting of GOSBA. She will be in Europe during that time.

Ms. Blews knows several members of your group and often cites the enthusiasm and dedication of those people.

Please extend your invitation again. Due to her busy schedule, I suggest six months' lead time, if your planning permits.

Sincerely

Marty Goebel
Secretary to Christine Blews

mtr

- Express regrets in first paragraph.
- When appropriate, give reasons for decision.
- Close with statement of good will.

REMINDER LETTER

May 15, 199—

Diane Shapiro
Clark County Vocational School
P.O. Box 345
Las Vegas, NV 89117

Dear Diane

At our June advisory meeting, each member was asked to bring 25 copies of publicity brochures distributed by the member's school to the September meeting. Please revise this request and bring 35 copies.

The mayor's office is sending a group of representatives to our meeting. We believe this will give our efforts an added boost.

It's been a very hot summer, so perhaps you will appreciate being reminded that the meeting is September 13, 12 noon, at the West Side Vocational School. A light lunch will be served.

Sincerely

Alfonso Torres
Chair

sw

- Refer to previous meeting, correspondence, or verbal agreement.
- State reason for letter.
- Provide any additional, pertinent information.

Suggested Solutions

■ **Chapter One**

Review & Practice (Pages 3-4)

Why was the letter written?
   To inform.

How well do you think the writer knows the reader?
   Not at all.

Does the letter convey a warm, human element?
   Yes.

What information was necessary?
   Invitation to speaker.
   Audience, date, time, and place.
   Information for response.

What results does the writer want?
   A positive response to the invitation.

Review & Practice (Page 6)

List the major points to be covered.
   1. Purpose for writing.
   2. Verification of date, time, place, event.
   3. Formal request to place in file.

Putting It All Together (Page 13)

Letter plan:
   1. Thank you.
   2. Information on product.
   3. Possible follow-through at later date.

87

Suggested Letter (Page 15)

Thank you for your inquiry regarding Version 2.1 of RapidWrite software.

The projected delivery date of V.2.1 is first quarter, 199–. While pricing information is not available at this time, we do not anticipate any major increases. Of course, experienced users like yourself will be able to upgrade from V.2.0 at a minimal cost.

You will be pleased to know that V.2.1 will include many of the enhancements suggested by our current users. Please continue to call our technical assistants at 1-800-225-5000 whenever you have a question or suggestion. Each one is important to us and is considered for future upgrades.

■ Chapter Two

Review & Practice (Page 21)

ABC Interoffice Memo

TO: Distribution List

FROM: Shirley Kyte

DATE: March 22, 199–

SUBJECT: IRS RULING—TRAVEL REIMBURSEMENT

On March 1, 199–, the IRS ruled (Opinion #345-QR) that all travel reimbursements must be included in the employee's tax forms as nontaxable compensation.

Please act immediately to add such reimbursements to the records of all employees to be included in the end-of-year reporting.

ert

Distribution:
A. Abrams
K. Chin
L. Jabbar
B. Kahookaulana

Review & Practice (Page 22)

List the major points to be covered.
1. The three new mailing deadlines.
2. Effective date.

Putting It All Together (Page 25)

Memo plan:
1. Details of presentation.
2. Notice to bring 12 copies of five-year department plans.

Suggested Memo (Page 26)

> The preliminary architectural plans for our expansion will be presented by Letitia Villacorta on Tuesday, March 15, at 9 A.M. in my office.
>
> Please bring 12 copies of your five-year department plans for distribution.

 # Chapter Three

Review & Practice (Page 38)

Conciseness
> Too many employees are taking extended coffee and lunch breaks.

Completeness
> Your performance review will be August 9 at 9:30 A.M. in Personnel A-25.

Courtesy
> When a good customer like you misses a payment, I know something is wrong.

Clarity
> A review of your substance abuse program will be conducted by members of UNLV's Wellness Division.

Correctness
> Four months have only 30 days: April, June, September, and November.

Chapter Review: Putting It All Together (Page 41)

February 1, 199–

Martin G. LeFavre
3301 Eastern Ave., Apt. 211
Wichita, KS 67215

Dear Martin

Thank you for applying for a sales position in our company. Unfortunately, we do not have any openings at this time.

Your file will remain active for a period of six months. If you wish to submit another application at that time, please send it to the attention of Kathryn O'Connor, Director of Human Resources.

Good luck in your job search!

Sincerely

■ Chapter Four

Review & Practice (Pages 48-49)

Use as Few Words as Possible
The current balance on your account is $259.95.

Eliminating Redundant Expressions
In my opinion, the attached statement contains the facts in the case.

Using Positive Words and Phrases
The enclosed brochure will help you understand why prompt payments are important.

Eliminating Cliches and Jargon
Thank you for helping us set our priorities.

Avoiding Sexist References
Employees hold their future within their own hands.

Review & Practice (Page 53)

Using Active Verbs
The new vacation policy, approved by the employee task force, gives employees of five or more years of service one additional week of vacation.

Avoiding a Condescending Tone

We continue to maintain our policy of payment due upon delivery, unless prior arrangements have been made.

Using Simple Words

Enclosed is a copy of Act #563 giving Kansas City homeowners the right to appeal property tax rates.

Review & Practice (Page 55)

Considering the Interests of the Reader

Please indicate on the enclosed postal card the color and size of the file cabinet you wish, and we will process your order immediately.

Paying Attention to Details

Each of the divisions has made a firm commitment to better quality control.

Chapter Review: Putting It All Together (Page 57)

February 20, 199–

Ara Godosian, Manager
ABC Suppliers Inc.
P.O. Box 4857
Newark, NJ 07152

Dear Mr. Godosian

Our records indicate that your account has been past due for five of the last six months. For that reason, all future sales must be on a cash basis.

You have been a good customer of long standing, and I am sorry to have to take this action. Because you and I have had an excellent business relationship, I have been granted one deviation from our company policy: Your credit account will be kept open for the next 10 days. If you wish to appeal our action, you may do so within that time.

Sincerely

Patrick Monaghan
Controller

■ Chapter Five

Review & Practice (Page 64)

What is the **capital** of Pennsylvania?

Marietta was recently promoted to **principal** of the school.

Sometimes we forget that it requires **some time** to learn to use new software.

Would we have **fewer** problems if we had **fewer** employees?

The **effect** of the devastating hurricane will **affect** hundreds of residents for many years.

Our goal is to **ensure** the success of the project.

If you had been given a choice **then,** would you have chosen to relocate rather **than** to stay?

How much **farther** do we have to drive?

I simply cannot **accept** the job offer at that salary.

We are **already** past our deadline. Are you **all ready** to defend our position?

Review & Practice (Pages 69-70)

Change in Tense
    The staff meeting began sharply at 9 A.M.; at 9:45 Concetta strolled in.

Agreement of Subject and Verb
    Neither the controller nor the analyst wants to change the current system.

Agreement of Pronoun and Antecedent
    Surgeons must be dedicated to their task.

Possessives
    When will your boss's monthly sales report be ready?

Chapter Review: Putting It All Together (Pages 71-72)

August 17, 199—

Marty Levitz, Managing Director
Showtime Theatricals
4556 East 56th Street
New York, NY 09056

Dear Marty

Thanks for confirming our commitment to participate in the December Festival of Lights. All our principal performers are already studying their roles. Your enthusiasm has captured us, too!

It's such an exciting time here. It is our privilege to be a sponsor of the Physically Challenged Children's Day events at Hyde Park on September 15. I recall that you have had a keen interest in this in the past. Julie was speaking at our planning session last Thursday when the lights went out. Never a dull moment—or a blank calendar!

Everyone sends regards. I'll be in touch very soon.

Sincerely

Esther Rabinowitz
Scheduling Director

jek

THE BUSINESS SKILLS EXPRESS SERIES

This growing series of books addresses a broad range of key business skills and topics to meet the needs of employees, human resource departments, and training consultants.

To obtain information about these and other Business Skills Express books, please call Business One IRWIN toll free at: 1-800-634-3966.